MYSTERIES OF SCIENCE

BIGFOOT

THE UNSOLVED MYSTERY

BY LISA WADE McCORMICK

Reading Consultant:
Barbara J. Fox
Reading Specialist
North Carolina State University

Content Consultant:
Michael Aragona
Field Researcher and Investigator
Bigfoot Field Researchers Organization

Capstone
press

Mankato, Minnesota

Books published by Capstone Press are manufactured with paper
containing at least 10 percent post-consumer waste.

Library of Congress Cataloging-in-Publication Data
McCormick, Lisa Wade, 1961–
    Bigfoot: the unsolved mystery/by Lisa Wade McCormick.
    p. cm. — (Blazers. Mysteries of science)
    Includes bibliographical references and index.
    Summary: "Presents the legend of Bigfoot, including current theories and famous
encounters"— Provided by publisher.
    ISBN-13: 978-1-4296-2326-1 (hardcover)
    ISBN-10: 1-4296-2326-8 (hardcover)
    1. Sasquatch — Juvenile literature. I. Title. II. Series.
QL89.2.S2M37 2009
001.944 — dc22   2008028700

Editorial Credits
Lori Shores, editor; Alison Thiele, designer; Marcie Spence, photo researcher

Photo Credits
Alamy/Dale O'Dell, 26–27
AP Images, cover
Corbis/Bettmann, 12–13, 22
Courtesy of Mike Aragona, BFRO Investigator New Jersey, 18–19, 23
Fortean Picture Library, 8–9, 11, 14, 28, 29
Getty Images Inc./Michael Turek, 4–5; VEER Antonino Barbagallo, 24–25
Mr. Randee Chase, 6–7
Newscom/Alf Wilson/Online USA, 15; Cindy Yamanaka/Orange County Register/MCT, 20–21
Shutterstock/Marilyn Volan, grunge background (throughout); Maugli, 16–17 (background);
    Schmeliova Natalia, 16 (paper art element); rgbspace, (paper art element) 3, 17

Printed in the United States of America in Stevens Point, Wisconsin.
012011
006049R

TABLE OF CONTENTS

A STRANGE SIGHT

A hiker sees a strange object
on a mountain in November 2005.
The object suddenly moves.

The hiker grabs his camera. He zooms in on a ridge of Silver Star Mountain. The hiker blinks in surprise.

The hiker sees a giant, hairy animal. It looks half man and half ape. Could it be the legendary bigfoot?

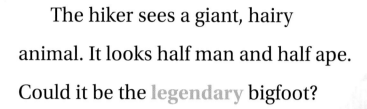

BIGFOOT FACT

Hairy, apelike animals have been seen in the Himalayan Mountains in Asia. People call these animals "yeti" or "abominable snowmen."

legendary — something that is part of a story handed down from earlier times

THE STORY OF BIGFOOT

For thousands of years, people have told stories of large **primates** roaming the woods. American Indians had many names for these animals. The Indian word *Sasquatch* means "wild man of the woods."

BIGFOOT FACT

Leif Eriksson wrote about seeing large primates in North America more than 1,000 years ago.

primate — any member of the group of intelligent animals that includes humans, apes, and monkeys

Many people believe they have seen a bigfoot. They say these large animals walk on two legs and are covered with dark hair.

BIGFOOT FACT

Bigfoots appear to be 7 to 10 feet (2 to 3 meters) tall. That is about as tall as a school bus.

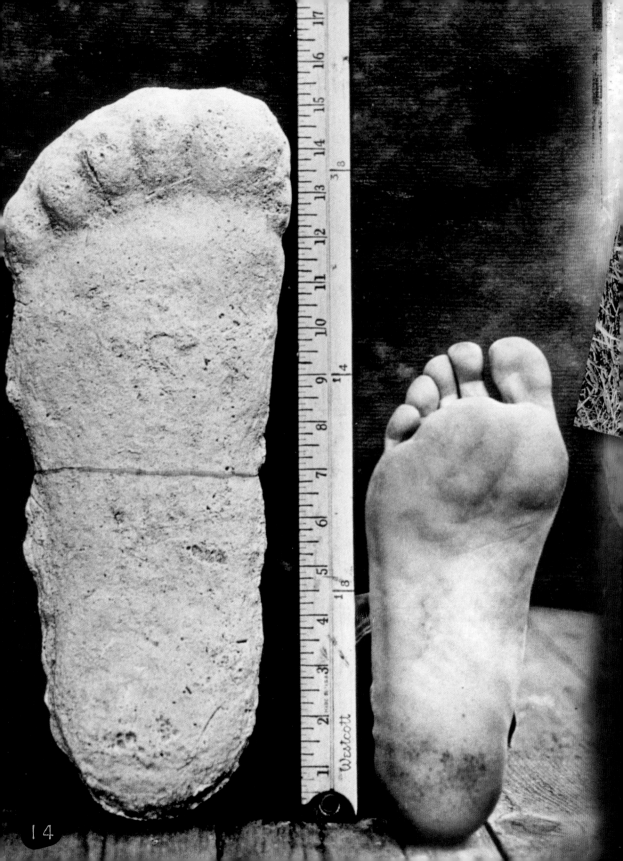

14

Many people find large footprints where a bigfoot was seen. Some footprints are more than 15 inches (38 centimeters) long.

FAMOUS ENCOUNTERS

In 2000, researchers found what could be the print of a bigfoot's body. The print seems to be the left forearm, hip, thigh, and heel of a large animal. Some scientists believe it was made by an unknown primate.

In 1995, a forest patrol officer in Washington said he saw a bigfoot. He grabbed his camera and took 14 pictures. But some people think the pictures are fake.

In 1967, Roger Patterson used a movie camera to take pictures of a bigfoot. The film shows the animal walking near a sandbar in Bluff Creek, California. No one has proven that the film is fake.

In 1924, Albert Ostman said bigfoots kidnapped him during a camping trip in Vancouver, Canada. Ostman said the bigfoots kept him for six days.

FINDING BIGFOOT

Bigfoot **researchers** hunt for clues deep in forests. They check areas where bigfoots were seen. They look for footprints and listen for strange sounds.

BIGFOOT FACT

The study of legendary animals is called cryptozoology (KRIP-toe-zoo-OL-uh-jee).

researcher — someone who studies a subject to discover new information

Researchers use special equipment to search for bigfoots. They use cameras that take pictures in the dark. Many researchers think bigfoots are most active at night.

Researchers have found hundreds of footprints they believe were made by bigfoots. They have recorded sounds they think the animals made.

BIGFOOT FACT

Researchers say bigfoots make odd howling and screaming sounds.

IS BIGFOOT REAL?

Many people think bigfoot is just a myth. No one has caught a bigfoot. No bigfoot bones have ever been found.

myth — a false idea that many people believe

25

Many people have taken pictures of bigfoots. But many pictures have turned out to be fake.

What do you think? Can researchers prove bigfoots are real?

29

GLOSSARY

legendary (LEJ-uhnd-air-ee) — something that is part of a story handed down from earlier times

myth (MITH) — a false idea that many people believe

primate (PRYE-mate) — any member of the group of intelligent animals that includes humans, apes, and monkeys

researcher (REE-surch-ur) — someone who studies a subject to discover new information

READ MORE

Shone, Rob. *Bigfoot and Other Strange Beasts.* Graphic Mysteries. New York: Rosen, 2006.

Teitelbaum, Michael. *Bigfoot Caught on Film: and Other Monster Sightings!* 24/7. New York: Franklin Watts, 2008.

Woog, Adam. *Bigfoot.* Encounters With. San Diego: KidHaven Press, 2006.

INTERNET SITES

FactHound offers a safe, fun way to find educator-approved Internet sites related to this book.

Here's what you do:

1. Visit *www.facthound.com*
2. Choose your grade level.
3. Begin your search.

This book's ID number is 9781429623261.

FactHound will fetch the best sites for you!

INDEX